OPRAH WINFREY

Media Superstar

Kristen Woronoff

BLACKBIRCH PRESS

Detroit • New York • San Diego • San Francisco
Boston • New Haven, Conn. • Waterville, Maine
London • Munich

Published by Blackbirch Press
10911 Technology Place
San Diego, CA 92127
e-mail: customerservice@galegroup.com
Web site: http://www.galegroup.com/blackbirch

© 2002 Blackbirch Press
an imprint of the Gale Group

Printed in China

10 9 8 7 6 5 4 3 2 1

Photo credits:
Cover © Getty images; cover inset, pages 3, 4, 7, 10-11, 13, 15, 16, 21, 24, 25, 27, 28, 29, 30 © CORBIS; page 9 © Arista Records, page 18-19 © photo by Irving Phillips, *The Baltimore Sun*; page 20, 22, 23, 42 © AP/Wide World Photos

Library of Congress Cataloging-in-Publication Data
Woronoff, Kristen.
Oprah Winfrey / by Kristen Woronoff.
        p. cm. — (Famous women juniors)
Summary: Introduces the life and career of Oprah Winfrey, the talk-show host who overcame her difficult childhood to win respect as a journalist, actress, and role model. Includes index.
        ISBN 1-56711-588-8 (alk. paper)
1. Winfrey, Oprah—Juvenile literature. 2. Television personalities—United States—Biography—Juvenile literature. 3. Motion picture actors and actresses—United States—Biography—Juvenile literature. [1. Winfrey, Oprah. 2. Television personalities. 3. Actors and actresses. 4. African Americans—Biography. 5. Women—Biography.] I. Title. II. Series.
PN1992.4.W56 W685 2002
791.45'028'092—dc21   2001005127

Everything about Oprah Winfrey's life started out wrong—even her name. Oprah's parents wanted to name her Orpah, after a name in the Bible. But the woman who delivered Oprah misspelled the name on the birth certificate. The woman wrote down Oprah instead of Orpah. Oprah is what the little girl was called.

Oprah was born on January 29, 1954, in Kosciusko, Mississippi. Her father was Vernon Winfrey. He was an army soldier. Her mother was Vernita Lee, an 18-year-old farm girl.

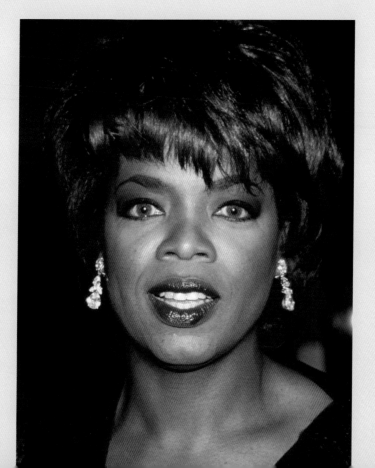

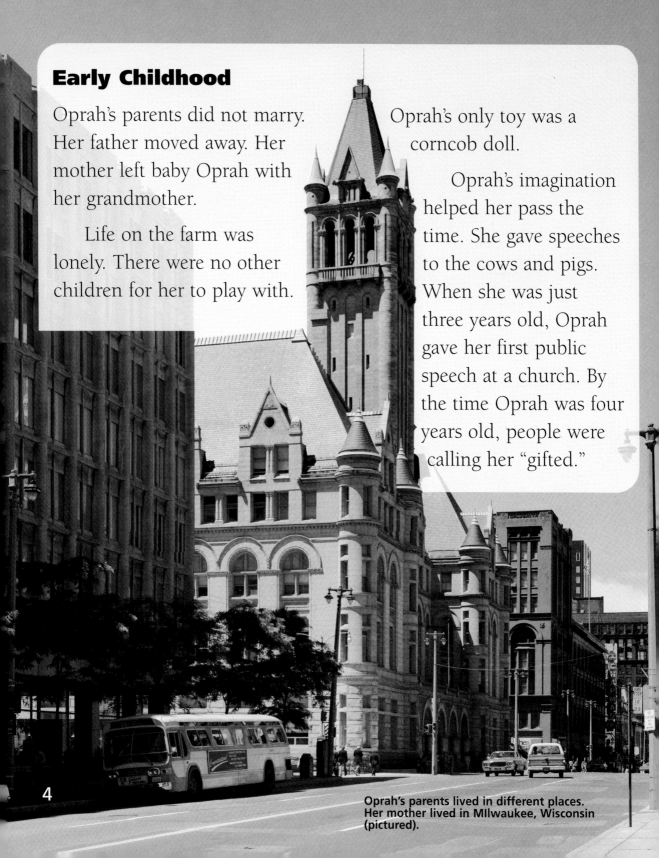

Early Childhood

Oprah's parents did not marry. Her father moved away. Her mother left baby Oprah with her grandmother.

Life on the farm was lonely. There were no other children for her to play with.

Oprah's only toy was a corncob doll.

Oprah's imagination helped her pass the time. She gave speeches to the cows and pigs. When she was just three years old, Oprah gave her first public speech at a church. By the time Oprah was four years old, people were calling her "gifted."

Oprah's parents lived in different places. Her mother lived in MIlwaukee, Wisconsin (pictured).

As young as she was, Oprah knew she was special. When she started kindergarten at the local school, she wrote a note to her teacher. It said: "Dear Miss New, I do not think I belong here." Miss New agreed. Oprah was placed in the first grade. After first grade, she went straight to the third grade.

Oprah's life changed a great deal after her sixth birthday. She began to spend time living with her parents. For three years, she traveled back and forth between her mother and her father. Her mother lived in Milwaukee, Wisconsin. Her father lived in Nashville, Tennessee.

Difficult Years

By the time she was eight, Oprah was a well-known speaker in school and at church. When she was nine years old, Oprah decided to live full-time with her mother and her two half brothers. The family lived in Milwaukee's poor black neighborhood. Oprah's mother worked long hours and did not have a lot of time for her daughter.

One day, while Oprah's mother was working, a terrible crime took place. Oprah's teenage cousin was babysitting her. The teenager forced Oprah to have sex. After the crime, the teenager said he would buy Oprah ice cream if she promised not to tell anyone.

Oprah has spoken publicly about the abuses she suffered as a child.

7

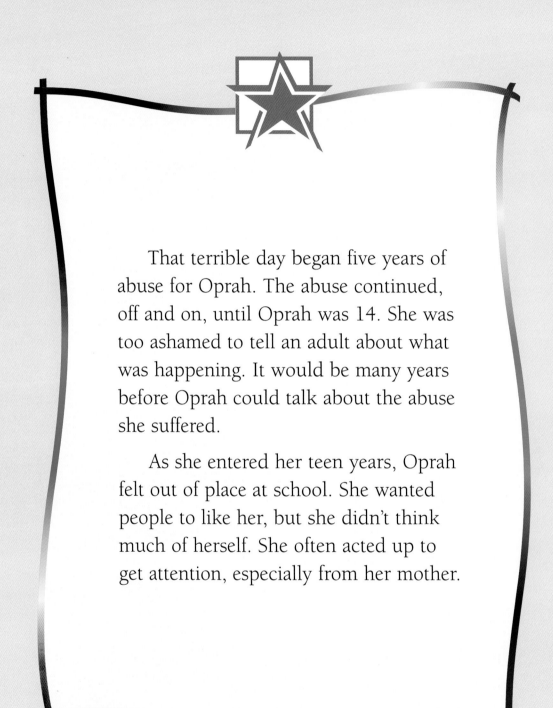

That terrible day began five years of abuse for Oprah. The abuse continued, off and on, until Oprah was 14. She was too ashamed to tell an adult about what was happening. It would be many years before Oprah could talk about the abuse she suffered.

As she entered her teen years, Oprah felt out of place at school. She wanted people to like her, but she didn't think much of herself. She often acted up to get attention, especially from her mother.

One day, Oprah saw the famous singer Aretha Franklin on the street. To get the star's attention, Oprah lied and said her parents had left her in Milwaukee. Oprah was so convincing, the singer gave her $1,000 to get home. Instead, Oprah got a hotel room and spent all the money. A local minister found out where she was and took her home to her mother.

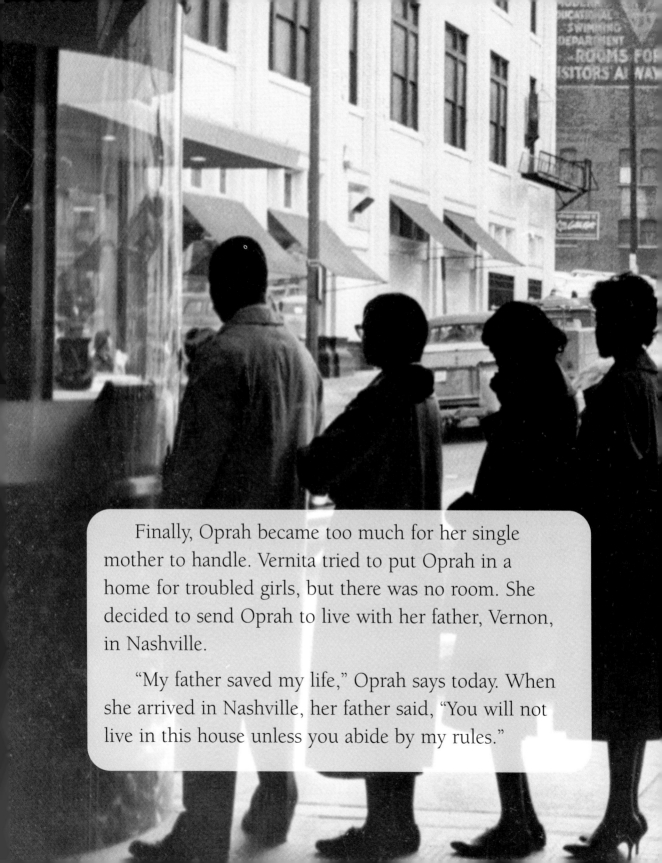

Finally, Oprah became too much for her single mother to handle. Vernita tried to put Oprah in a home for troubled girls, but there was no room. She decided to send Oprah to live with her father, Vernon, in Nashville.

"My father saved my life," Oprah says today. When she arrived in Nashville, her father said, "You will not live in this house unless you abide by my rules."

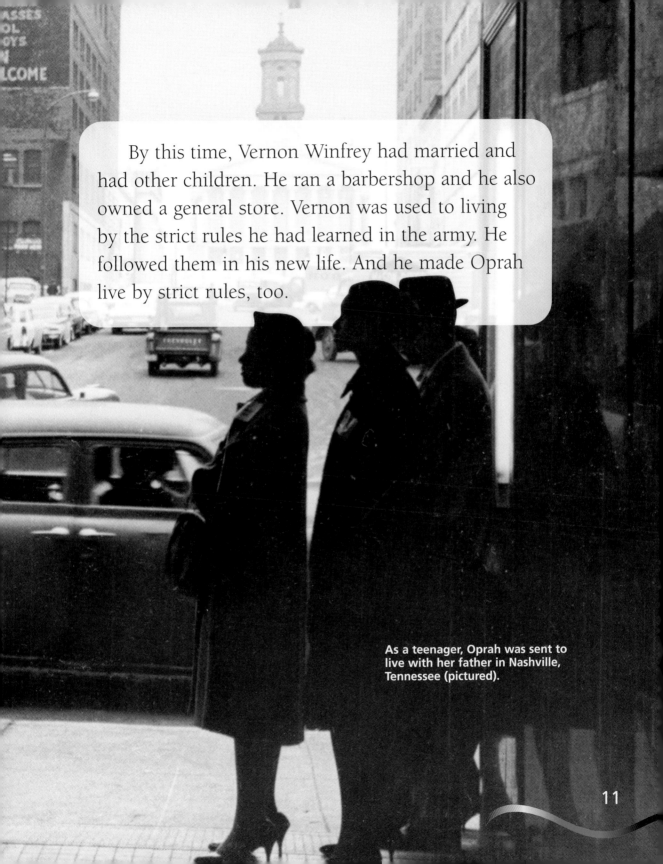

By this time, Vernon Winfrey had married and had other children. He ran a barbershop and he also owned a general store. Vernon was used to living by the strict rules he had learned in the army. He followed them in his new life. And he made Oprah live by strict rules, too.

As a teenager, Oprah was sent to live with her father in Nashville, Tennessee (pictured).

Living with her father meant Oprah had to change. Just getting C's in school was not good enough. She had to make the honor roll. Vernon also made Oprah learn five new words every day. If she didn't, she would not get any dinner. She had to read one book every week and write a report on it for her father. She was allowed to watch television for only one hour each day.

The difficult rules changed Oprah's life. She earned good grades. She became a leader in school. At 16, she won a public-speaking contest in Nashville. The prize was a full scholarship to Tennessee State University.

Once, while working on a school project, Oprah asked people to sponsor her for a walkathon. She asked John Heidelberg, a disc jockey at WVOL radio in Nashville, to be a sponsor.

The disc jockey liked Oprah's smooth way with words. He wanted her to make a practice tape for the radio station's owners. It wasn't long before she had a job at the radio station. Though she was only a teenager, Oprah read the radio news after school and on weekends.

Oprah's smooth voice and easy manner made her perfect for radio.

As she began to feel better about herself, Oprah entered a beauty contest. She didn't consider herself beautiful and still doesn't. But to her surprise, she won. Within a few years, the troubled girl had become an honor student, a radio announcer, and a contest winner.

Oprah continued working at the radio station after she graduated from high school. She wanted to move away, but her father would not let her. Instead, she attended Tennessee State University. It was not a happy time in her life. Racism and prejudice were at their height. Many young people at the all-black school took part in political protests. Oprah did not, and she felt out of place. "I hated, hated, hated college," Oprah once said.

Oprah's college years were a difficult time for America. Racism and prejudice were everywhere. Here, civil rights activists speak at a rally.

Oprah has always known that she wanted to be a journalist and entertainer.

Oprah continued to enter beauty contests while in college. She hoped to use the prize money to pay for her education. During the Miss Black Nashville pageant, Oprah was asked what she wanted to do with her life. She told the judges: "I believe in truth. So I want to be a journalist." She won the pageant.

A Career in Television

Oprah then got a great opportunity. A person from the local TV station in Nashville was at one of Oprah's pageants. The station asked her to apply for a job as their first African-American news announcer. At first, Oprah did not want to do it. But friends told her that it was a chance that she couldn't turn down.

Oprah was happily surprised when she got the job. At age 22, she was a rising star in radio and TV. But she still lived at home under the strict rules of her father. Oprah loved her father, but she knew it was time to leave.

By luck, a job offer came from a TV station in Baltimore, Maryland. It was a good position. Plus, she was able to move out of her father's house. Oprah jumped at the chance to be on her own.

The new TV job seemed like the answer to Oprah's dreams.

Oprah worked as a reporter at WJZ-TV in Baltimore, Maryland.

Billboards were put up around Baltimore announcing her arrival. She would be famous. But in a big city, being a news reporter was different from what Oprah was used to. She wanted to be emotional and give her feelings about news stories. Once, when she interviewed a woman whose children had been killed in a fire, Oprah began to cry on TV. News reporters were not supposed to show their feelings. The station management began to think that Oprah was the wrong person for the job.

In April 1977, Oprah was taken off the six o'clock news. But she had a contract, so the station had to keep her. Station owners decided to have her announce news in the morning.

Finally, something happened that changed Oprah's career. The station began a morning talk show to compete with the popular *Phil Donahue Show*. The new show was called *People Are Talking*. Oprah was picked to host the show.

Oprah wanted to be a reporter, but she was surprised to find she liked hosting a talk show.

At first, Oprah wasn't excited about the job. She wanted to be a news reporter. But on her first day, she discovered that she felt at home. She could laugh and joke and just be herself—feelings and all. Viewers liked Oprah, too. She hosted the show for six years.

After those six years, Oprah was ready for a change. She applied for a position at *A.M. Chicago*, another talk show. She got the job and moved to Chicago in 1983.

Oprah and two television executives talk about the syndication of her show, *A.M. Chicago*.

On *A.M. Chicago*, Oprah had many different guests. And soon, her show was more popular than *The Phil Donahue Show*. Oprah did not prepare her questions. She just asked what she wanted to know. And audiences liked her style. There were times, however, when Oprah was nervous. Talking to famous artists or movie stars sometimes made Oprah feel like a tongue-tied young girl from Nashville. But even at these times, viewers loved her. They knew they would feel nervous and tongue-tied in her place.

A.M. Chicago became so popular, it was changed from 30 minutes long to an hour. The name was also changed to *The Oprah Winfrey Show*. Oprah and her manager worked to have the show syndicated. That meant it would be seen all over the country instead of just in Chicago.

Oprah has always been popular with her fans because of her honesty.

In September 2000, Oprah interviewed presidential candidate Al Gore.

    Soon, *The Oprah Winfrey Show* was the most popular show on television. Audiences loved Oprah's honesty. On one show, Oprah finally told the entire audience her dark secret about the abuse she had suffered as a child. After the show, many people called her to say they understood her pain. Oprah's courage helped others speak about abuse they had suffered.

Oprah interviewed pop star
Michael Jackson in 1983.

Movies, Book Clubs, and Romance

By now, Oprah was a national TV star. She was also very rich. She had moved into a fancy apartment and was a millionaire by the age of 32.

Even though she was successful on TV, Oprah still had other goals. Since her childhood, she had wanted to be an actress. She had acted in college plays. Once she left school, however, she did not think about acting.

Oprah had a featured role in the movie *The Color Purple*.

One day, musician Quincy Jones saw Oprah's show and asked her to be in a movie called *The Color Purple*. Oprah was very excited. *The Color Purple* was one of her favorite books. She took the part. After that, she acted in other roles as well.

On September 8, 1991, Oprah's show became one of the highest-rated programs in television history.

But Oprah showed people that she was more than just a TV star. She has always helped with social causes. And she is extremely generous. Oprah has given coworkers and relatives fur coats, money, and all-expense-paid vacations. She also spends a lot of time speaking at homeless shelters and churches.

Oprah makes many public appearances in support of social causes.

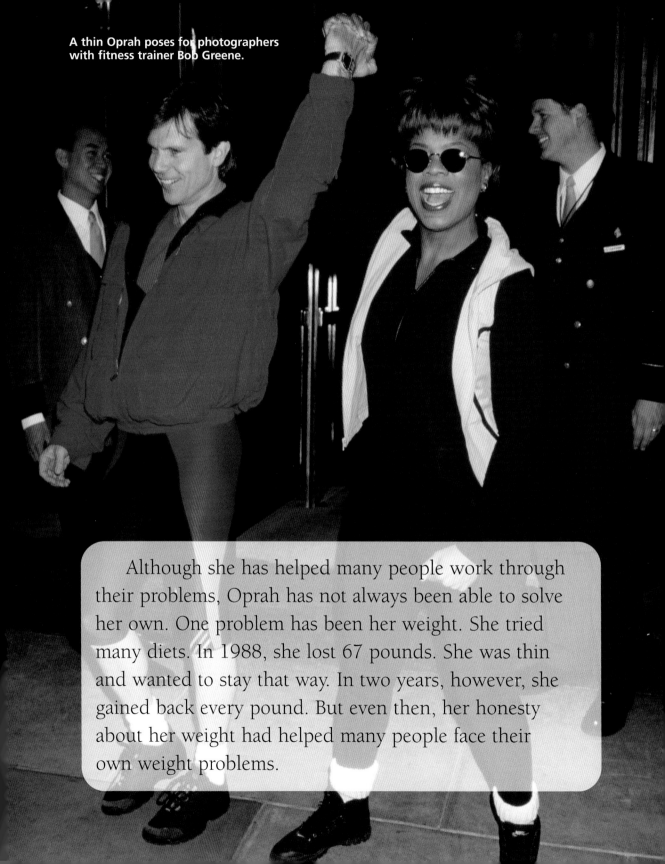

A thin Oprah poses for photographers with fitness trainer Bob Greene.

Although she has helped many people work through their problems, Oprah has not always been able to solve her own. One problem has been her weight. She tried many diets. In 1988, she lost 67 pounds. She was thin and wanted to stay that way. In two years, however, she gained back every pound. But even then, her honesty about her weight had helped many people face their own weight problems.

Over the years, Oprah has built on the success of her show. In 1998, she began using part of her show to talk about books that she had read. Soon she started "Oprah's Book Club." Each month, Oprah picks a book that she has enjoyed and talks about it with guests and the book's author. Her show has helped sell thousands of books. Oprah has also started a magazine and her own cable TV channel. And she has become one of the wealthiest people in the United States.

Television journalist Barbara Walters (left) and singer Diana Ross (right) attended the party to celebrate Oprah's new magazine.

Future president George W. Bush appeared on Oprah's show during his campaign for office.

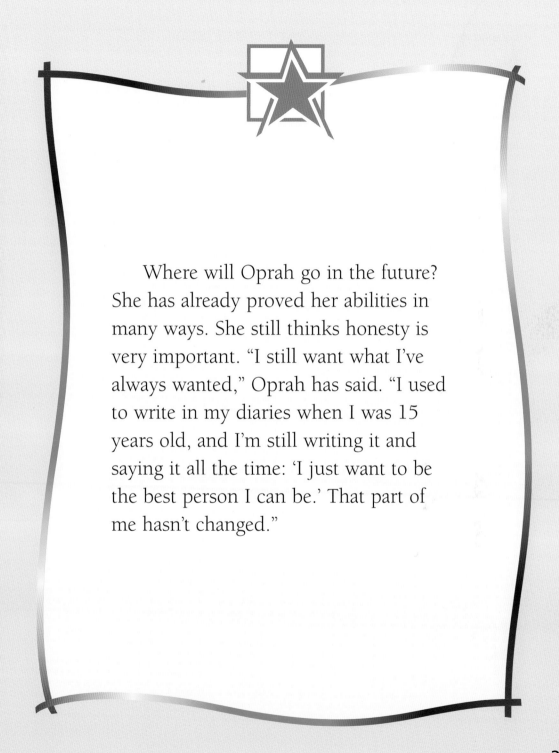

Where will Oprah go in the future? She has already proved her abilities in many ways. She still thinks honesty is very important. "I still want what I've always wanted," Oprah has said. "I used to write in my diaries when I was 15 years old, and I'm still writing it and saying it all the time: 'I just want to be the best person I can be.' That part of me hasn't changed."

Glossary

Abide To accept, or conform to.

Abuse Improper use or treatment.

Gifted Talented.

Journalist A writer or editor for a news source.

Neighborhood A group of people living near one another.

Pageant A show or contest.

Prejudice Negative attitude toward a person or group of people based on race or some other characteristic.

Protest A public complaint or rejection of a policy or standard.

Racism Belief that race determines a person's capabilities and station in life.

Sponsor A person or organization who pays for a project.

Strict Severe in discipline.

For More Information

Websites

The Oprah Winfrey Show
www.oprah.com

A comprehensive Oprah Winfrey website, mostly having to do with her television show.

The Hall of Business: Oprah Winfrey
www.achievement.org/autodoc/page/win0pro-1

Website includes a biography and an interview with Oprah.

Books

Friedrich, Belinda. *Oprah Winfrey*. Broomall, PA: Chelsea House, 2001.

Presnall, Judith Janda. *Oprah Winfrey* (People in the News). San Diego: Lucent Books, 1999.

Stone, Tanya Lee. *Oprah Winfrey : Success With an Open Heart*. Brookfield, CT: Millbrook Press, 2001.

Index